Ministering Freedom
to the Emotionally Wounded

Doris M. Wagner,
General Editor

WAGNER
PUBLICATIONS

Ministering Freedom to the Emotionally Wounded
Copyright © 2003 by Doris M. Wagner
ISBN 1-58502-034-6
Library of Congress Control Number: 2003102723

Published by
Wagner Publications
11005 N. Highway 83
Colorado Springs, CO 80921
www.wagnerpublications.org

Cover design by
Imagestudios
100 East St. Suite 105
Colorado Springs, CO 80903
719-578-0351   www.imagestudios.net

Edit by C. Lil Walker
Interior design by Rebecca Sytsema

Rights for publishing this book in other languages are contracted by Gospel Literature International (GLINT). GLINT also provides technical help for the adaptation, translation, and publishing of Bible study resources and books in scores of languages worldwide. For further information, contact GLINT, P.O. Box 4060, Ontario, CA 91761-1003, USA. You may also send e-mail to glintint@aol.com, or visit their web site at www.glint.org.

1   2   3   4   5   6   7   8   9   09   08   07   06   05   04   03

Contents

Meet the Contributors

While most Christians believe that demons exist somewhere in the world, a relatively small number of Christians realize that demons can affect their daily lives; and even fewer know how to effectively deal with one. But that is changing! Over the past few decades there has been a great resurgence in both the understanding and practice of deliverance. Because there is a need to understand this type of ministry, I decided to offer a useful series of books to help both the local church and the average Christian be equipped to effectively minister freedom from demonic oppression. Each book in the series will deal with a specific topic. In this second book of the series, I have gathered experts in the field of deliverance to the emotionally wounded who will explain how demons can take advantage of our emotions and the traumatic experiences in our lives, as well as give practical advice for ministering deliverance. I'd like to briefly introduce each of them to you:

Doris M. Wagner

Unforgiveness is one of the greatest obstacles to peace and deliverance in many lives. It is the one thing that Satan seems to take the most advantage of to keep people in bondage. For that reason I have written this chapter, with the hopes that many will be able to forgive even that which seems unforgivable, and thereby be set free to live the life God intended for them.

Cindy Jacobs

Cindy has been a very dear friend for many years. I have learned a great deal about deliverance from her. Her teaching on releasing bitter root judgments has been a key teaching that has helped many people. In this chapter Cindy explains how the principle of reaping and sowing actually binds us and those around us to the bitter root judgments we have made and how to we can be set free.

Chris Hayward

Chris has the clearest teaching on rejection that I have ever heard. It has been a great help to thousands. As he explains in his chapter, to the degree that we embrace rejection in our lives, we are unable to receive love, even from God. Chris defines the four walls of rejection and offers concrete steps and prayers to see the walls broken down in our lives.

John L. Sandford

John Sandford, along with his wife, Paula, are true pioneers in the field of deliverance and inner healing. This book would not have been complete without a contribution from John. In his chapter he deals specifically with the issues of fear and anger giving key insights into ministering freedom to those who are bound by them.

Peter Horrobin

Peter has some of the plainest and most understandable teaching on every facet of deliverance. He gave a talk on how trauma affects the whole person in one of our seminars a few years ago and I was shocked to see how many people had been affected by trauma and needed ministry. Peter has duplicated that teaching in his chapter, and I know you'll benefit from reading it.

Dale M. Sides

So many have suffered from various forms of victimization and trauma which leaves, as Dale explains, cracks in the soul and fragmentation in our lives. In his chapter, Dale offers a very sound and innovative teaching on the two-step remedy for mending these cracks in the soul and bringing wholeness to our lives.

Chapter One

Forgiving the Unforgivable

Doris M. Wagner

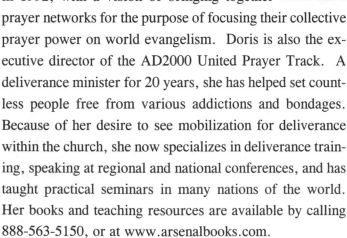

Doris Wagner along with her husband, C. Peter Wagner, founded Global Harvest Ministries in 1992, with a vision of bringing together prayer networks for the purpose of focusing their collective prayer power on world evangelism. Doris is also the executive director of the AD2000 United Prayer Track. A deliverance minister for 20 years, she has helped set countless people free from various addictions and bondages. Because of her desire to see mobilization for deliverance within the church, she now specializes in deliverance training, speaking at regional and national conferences, and has taught practical seminars in many nations of the world. Her books and teaching resources are available by calling 888-563-5150, or at www.arsenalbooks.com.

I wasn't ministering deliverance over people very long before I began hearing heartbreaking stories from those whom I was trying to help. Most of these men and women were suffering from varying degrees of emotional wounding inflicted by others. Some of the wounding seemed intentional and some was not; but the fact remained that these people were often severely emotionally crippled and were not able to be all that God wanted them to be at the time.

Rejection

Wounding from others usually results in some form of rejection. I hope you take the time to read carefully Chris Hayward's chapter on rejection. It is a tool that Satan frequently uses to inflict damage to individuals, both Christian and non-Christian alike. Rejection can be severe in many cases. For example, a person can experience rejection because they were an unwanted child. They know it and it hurts.

Often adopted children suffer severe rejection and a feeling of abandonment which causes these youngsters frequently to become rebellious, difficult young people. They are plagued by the question: "Why didn't my parents want me?" They are wounded, even though love is lavished on them by their adoptive parents. A demon of rejection often enters this wounding and makes their lives miserable.

Other common forms of rejection show up due to negative circumstances at home or at school: a divorce, a bad job situation, financial disaster, a physical handicap, an accident resulting in disfigurement, and so on. As a result of these difficult circumstances, people often feel unwanted, unloved, unlucky, or any number of other things. They sometimes blame themselves or others and, as a result, emotional wounding takes place.

Deliberate Sin

Deliberate sin can lead to all sorts of problems and invitations to demons that leave emotional wounding. I pray for many who have lamented, "How could I have done such a thing?" Some have sought out false religions and were tempted to do very bad things, resulting in depression, anxiety, and even sexual disease and mental problems. It is a very good idea to abide by the Ten Commandments and New Testament teaching. It saves all sorts of emotional problems.

Sexual Abuse

Many times, sources of severe emotional wounding have to do with sexual issues. I recall having heard over the radio about a certain court case in the State of California when we lived there during the decade of the 1980s. I do not recall if there was a jury in this case, but probably not, because the female judge passed the ruling in this instance. I wish the judge had been Judge Judy, because she certainly would have done a far better job on this one. It involved the case of a 12-year-old girl who had been raped. This particular judge let the man who raped her go free because, in her words, "the girl had not been harmed."

I have prayed over a number of rape victims and let me assure you that a person who has been raped, be it male or female, has, indeed, been seriously harmed both physically and emotionally. Life is never the same. The devil often uses such horrible experiences to open many doors to demonic intrusion. Not all cases are alike, but I have frequently had to deal with a long string of demons including several of the following: trauma, lust, fear, anger, hatred, rejection, self-rejection, self-hatred, a man- or woman-hating spirit, a God-hating spirit, pornography, worthlessness, and in extreme cases, prostitution, abortion, death, suicide, homosexuality, lesbianism, bestiality, and on and on. It is just not a pretty picture.

I get particularly upset and especially angry at the devil when sexual abuse happens to children. I can hardly speak about it without crying. Recently a number of these stories have hit the media in great detail. If you have read the accounts of these victims, you see that many of them suffered emotional shipwreck. The wickedness of those who committed the sins and crimes have, in some cases, transferred on to the victims. "Abused people abuse" and "Hurt people hurt people" are phrases that so often hold true in these cases. Those who were sexually abused will sometimes abuse others in the same way. Some victims will report symptoms such as night-mares, failed marriages, fears in many forms, despair, anxi-ety, severe depression, uncontrollable anger and rage, lust, pornography, and all manner of sexual sin. Some have even committed suicide. And the picture gets uglier.

Sexual abuse is just one form of victimization, and I have spent quite a bit of time on it because it is common. Although I hate to say it, it seems to be on the rise. I firmly believe that the growing acceptance by the public of raunchy television, movies, and printed and internet porn contribute to "copycat" activity as well as providing frequent openings for a spirit of lust to invade those who are "fascinated" in or take part in such activity. When the conservative Christians kick and scream about protecting our children from these things, as I recently read, those of a more liberal mindset bemoan the fact that we "...just don't understand the First Amendment!" How sad for them, and for us!

The Occult

People, often children, who have been forcefully introduced into witchcraft or Satanism, with the accompanying rituals, have frequently fallen victim to prolonged, paralyzing fear and unspeakable pain or, in some cases, torture. These wounded emotions are openings for demons to further torment the vic-tims. Trauma, anger, witchcraft, lust, rejection of the most vile form, depression, and a host of other emotional ailments sometimes erupt, each bringing its own set of demons. These people were victimized and their lives have been greatly harmed as a result.

It is so difficult for me to even imagine anyone wanting to hurt a child or subject a child or young person to something that they know will have severe and long lasting physical and emotional consequences. Animals do not treat their

> The devil wants to tell us that we have a right to hang on to unforgiveness, and by the world's standards, we probably do. But we are not of the world – we are citizens of heaven and as such, we have the power to forgive the unforgivable.

young like that! Perhaps the only reasonable explanation is a fallen, sinful nature accompanied by help from Satan and his demons.

If a person comes from a background of witchcraft or Satanism, and finds Christ as his or her Savior, I have found that these severely emotionally wounded individuals sometimes become angry with the person or persons who have victimized them. Unforgiveness can set in and become a demonic stronghold in their lives.

Bitterness, Resentment, Hatred, Anger

Unforgiveness is often accompanied by four other demon buddies: bitterness, resentment, hatred, and anger. On top of the emotional wounding that was inflicted, the person then suffers from this additional anguish, making matters even more miserable. Peace and happiness evade them; relationships fail terribly.

A pivotal question to ask might be: Does the person have reason to be angry, bitter, confused, or hurt? Of course! The person has been victimized by others, and the victimization was spurred on by Satan – he who has come to steal, kill, and destroy. And much has, indeed, been stolen, destroyed, and killed. Perhaps the perpetrator is a relative or some other dangerous individual who is not in jail – justice has not been done and helplessness is added to the anger, bitterness, confusion, and hurt.

Christ Can Heal

It would be wonderful if all of these problems were totally wiped away at conversion, but the reality of the matter is that sometimes they linger on and rob the new Christian of joy. Is Christ capable of healing wounds so severe? Has He already paid the price? Must the new Christian take steps to appropriate more freedom? What keeps the wounding from being totally healed in all cases? These questions keep coming from good people who are trying to understand. The answers are always the same.

Of course Christ is entirely able to heal wounds so severe. Yes, He has already paid the full price. As for freedom, I have found that the key usually lies in forgiveness. In those cases where total freedom does not come at conversion, a session of forgiveness and inner healing almost always brings full release and freedom.

The Bondage of Unforgiveness

I titled this chapter "Forgiving the Unforgivable." Some atrocities and horrible sins against children, women, and the helpless seem unforgivable, humanly speaking. But we are "not of this world" and we are commanded to forgive, even though it is a difficult thing to do.

You see, unforgiveness is a bondage. A bondage is like an invisible rope that ties things together, usually in a knot. But the good news is that the bondage can be severed and there can be total freedom. Even more exciting is that this freedom often extends to the sometimes vile person who is to blame, as well as to the person who does the forgiving. I have seen circumstances shift dramatically as a person forgave someone of a terrible injustice. It is somewhat akin to being let out of jail.

There are two often-overlooked aspects of forgiveness. First, to extend forgiveness to a person does not imply condoning the sin, injustice, hurt or even the crime committed by that person. It simply releases the parties held by the bondage. Perhaps I can explain this aspect more easily.

Dying Well

I had to wait for some lab work to be done in a hospital a few months ago. This was a fine, large hospital and many had come to have blood drawn, or for other sorts of tests. Since the waiting room was crowded, I began to look around for something to read and discovered that the hospital had produced a variety of pamphlets for the varying needs of their patients and families. The one that interested me at the time was one entitled "Preparing to Die Well." So I picked it up and read what it had to say to those with terminal illness.

My husband, Peter, and I had shortly before held a "family conference" with our three daughters and their husbands to discuss a bit of our thinking concerning the time that is sure to come when we are both gone. We discussed a number of things, but we soon discovered that something our girls dearly wanted us to do ourselves was to prearrange our own funerals. One of our girls just burst into tears and begged, "Please don't make me pick out your casket!"

It was then that we realized that it would be a favor for our kids not to saddle them with all of those arrangements at a time of deep grief, when we could do it ourselves and pre-pay all of the expenses. Everything is done. We even chose our matching caskets (perhaps appropriately named "Mission" since mission has characterized our lives), our grave plot, and headstone which is engraved, up, and ready. Only the dates of death need to be added when the time comes. So now our girls each have two phone numbers to call when the time comes: the funeral agency and the lawyer who has our wills. We have been profusely thanked by our family.

Thinking that the pamphlet had to do with those sorts of arrangements, I was very pleasantly surprised to read that it went much further and gave some very sound and practical advice. I would like to quote a paragraph from this pamphlet entitled "Preparing to Die Well" by Kay Talbot, Ph.D.

"Planning your funeral, writing a will, resolving spiritual questions, and saying good-byes are important ways of expressing your individuality, communicating your final wishes, and leaving a legacy for loved ones. To complete your unfinished business and find serenity, you may need to forgive and/or be forgiven. Forgiving does not mean condoning insensitive or abusive behavior, or trusting those who are not trustworthy. Forgiving is something you do for yourself to find peace; it dissolves anger like an antacid. It is a way of looking at others as being unable to love and cherish you in the ways you needed. You forgive the person, not the act. Those who ask and receive forgiveness from others, from God, and from themselves, become able to live their remaining days with greater freedom than ever before. Forgiveness sets your spirit free."

This is one of the most eloquent treatments of the subject of forgiveness I have seen. I certainly hope many persons, not only the terminally ill, will take the advice to heart!

Making the Right Choices

Probably the second most important aspect is that forgiveness is a choice. Actually, it is a command from our Lord and Savior Jesus Christ; but we as individuals have the option of obeying or disobeying that command, because we have been given a free will to make choices. Making choices often entails living with the consequences of those choices.

The most familiar passage of Scripture that teaches forgiveness is Matthew 6:9-15, commonly known as *The Lord's Prayer*. When the disciples asked Jesus to teach them to pray, He told them to pray the Lord's Prayer, containing the phrase in verse 12 (I am using the New King James version), "Forgive our debts as we forgive our debtors." Some versions translate this verse "Forgive us our trespasses as we forgive those who trespass against us." After the prayer is completed, Jesus goes back and elaborates on verse 12, as though to underscore it as being very important. He says in verses 14 and 15: "For if you forgive men their trespasses, your heavenly Father will also forgive you. But if you do not forgive men their trespasses, neither will your Father forgive your trespasses." It seems clear that unforgiveness can lock a person in prison.

I often deal with people who feel that their sin is too great to be forgiven, and they feel very unworthy. Or, they feel as though the wretched sins committed against them are so grievous that it is impossible for them to forgive others because their lives have been all but ruined. This, of course, is exactly what Satan whispers in their ears and wants them to believe. He wants them to be locked in the prison of unforgiveness and to lock others in an adjoining cell. But, thanks be to God, He came to "proclaim freedom for the prisoners" (Luke 4:18 NIV).

Forgiveness Can Be Difficult

When we come to a point in a deliverance session where I can clearly see that the person I am praying with needs to forgive someone who has committed a sin, an injustice, a false accusation, a betrayal, an abuse, or even a crime, we simply pause and I ask the person to pray to the Lord and extend forgiveness to the person at fault. Sometimes it is very difficult. I then underscore the fact that what we are thereby doing is bringing freedom to both persons involved. I often encourage the person to pray a prayer something like

"As Christ forgave me all my sin, I choose to forgive (person's name) for (sin committed)." Forgiveness is a choice. Forgiveness is obedience to Jesus Christ. Forgiveness is usually a key to freedom. This freedom is a freedom from the bondage that has tied one person to the sin of another, possibly for years.

A Demon of Unforgiveness

When an injustice or serious sin has been committed, such as sexual abuse against a child, the child remembers the pain, the violation, the trauma, the panic, the very breath being denied him or her, and visits that situation over and over again in his or her mind. Unforgiveness sets in and eventually invites a demon of unforgiveness to set up housekeeping in the soul of that person. What that demon has acquired is the legal right to be there, because it is feeding off of the injustice and the repeated visitation to that event. It can become very entrenched.

However, when a person extends forgiveness, the legal right of that demon to stay has been removed and it must leave when commanded to do so in the name of Jesus Christ. Sometimes these demons put up a fight to stay or they may even say that they don't have to leave (which is a lie). Their legal right to remain has been knocked out by forgiveness. Of course all of the other traumas need to be prayed over and corresponding demons must be expelled as they are encountered. But as each one is expelled, the power of the remaining demons is that much weaker as their evil confederation begins to disintegrate. Then serious, concentrated prayer for the healing of memories needs to take place. Be sure to digest Dale Sides' chapter on mending cracks in the soul in this book. It is a valuable resource in the healing of memories due to trauma.

"I Hate His Guts!"

Let me tell you a dramatic story of a woman I was praying for who had some unforgiveness with which she was dealing. She had some strong disagreements with her husband that concerned household finances. In her own words: "I hated my husband and had contacted an attorney to get a divorce. I became suicidal and was hospitalized. I had family problems." Their finances were extremely stretched and they owed $5,000 in income tax, due in about a month. Because the problem seemed to be mostly the husband's fault, I asked her to forgive him. She answered me, with all the venom she could spew, "I hate his guts!" So I told her to go home and ask God to help her come to the place where she could choose to forgive him. About two weeks later I got a call from her with a simple phrase: "I can forgive, now." She came back and we prayed. She was able to forgive her husband. We prayed and cast out demons of unforgiveness and hatred along with some others.

When she left, we asked God to supply that enormous need of $5,000. I got a phone call from her just a couple of days later. I love these phone calls that start out with the phrase, "You'll never guess what happened!" She went on to say that she had been awakened at 7 a.m. (we were in California at the time) by a phone call from the East Coast Disability Insurance office. She had applied for disability due to a serious illness two years previously, but had never heard back from them. The person on the other end of the phone said that the application papers had literally fallen between two desks and had just been recovered. That day they were placing in the mail a check in the amount of $5,000 for back disability payments. I am sure there was a cause and effect in operation here. Forgiveness is a powerful weapon against the devil, and I believe that in this case God honored that step of obedience; and to show how much He was pleased with it, He honored her by immediately supplying her pressing need.

I received a note from her a few weeks later that said, "The hate for my husband is gone. Every day I pray and look for ways to please him. Our family is healing. Things turned around 180°. We are excited for each new day to see what God does." A letter like this to a weary deliverance worker suddenly erases the weariness and gives new strength to continue on.

Don't Put It Off

We cannot entertain unforgiveness even for a day. Scripture commands us not to let the sun go down on our anger (Ephesians 4:26). Why? Because it gets worse with time and might give an opening for demonic activity. It is good to think of unforgiveness as a luxury that we cannot afford.

We have in our power the ability to forgive because it was given to us as Christians by our Lord. Obedience is the key, and the sooner it is used, the better. The devil wants to tell us that we have a right to hang on to unforgiveness, and by the world's standards, we probably do. But we are not of the world – we are citizens of heaven and as such, we have the power to forgive the unforgivable. The words of Jesus are truth and by knowing the truth and being obedient to it, we can then be assured that we "shall know the truth and the truth shall make you free.... If the Son makes you free, you shall be free indeed" (John 8:30-36). No longer in bondage, no longer in pain, no longer a victim, but free indeed. I like that!

Chapter Two

Releasing Bitter Root Judgments

Cindy Jacobs

Widely recognized as a prophet to the nations, Cindy Jacobs is the president and cofounder of Generals of Intercession, an international missionary organization devoted to training in prayer and spiritual warfare. The global headquarters for Generals of Intercession is located in Colorado Springs, CO, where Mike and Cindy currently reside. In addition to being a widely recognized speaker, Cindy is the author of several books including the best-selling *Possessing the Gates of the Enemy*, *The Voice of God*, and *Women of Destiny*. She also edited and produced the *Women of Destiny Bible*. These and others of her resources are available through Generals of Intercession by calling 719-535-0977 or visiting www.generals.org.

One day my husband, Mike, came home from his job at American Airlines in Dallas, Texas, with a shocking announcement—we were going to sell our house and he was going back to school! This was very strange behavior from my husband. For one, we never just made unilateral decisions like that without consulting one another. For another, he had always told me that he had no reason to get his Master's in Business for his job.

That night I tried to reason with him; all to no avail. "Mike," I presented, "let's pray about this together and get the mind of the Lord." However, there was no budging him— the house was to go on the market and we were going to use all of our money for his schooling.

The next morning I set aside time to prayerfully ask the Lord what He was trying to say through this. I really wanted to inquire of God to find out who had kidnapped my husband and replaced him with this alien. As I sat still, I tried to quiet my fuming spirit. My thoughts were churning with statements to God that ran the gamut from, "How dare he be so arrogant," to, "Lord, he's not living with me in a loving and kind way."

At last I settled down enough for the Lord to really speak to my heart. He whispered to me, "Cindy, Mike is being unreasonable, isn't he?" Sensing that I would only get my self into deeper trouble than I was already in for my bad attitude, I sat very still and listened. At last He said, "You are reaping what you have sown."

Right then, I had a picture of myself as a little child, sitting in a car full of our household goods with my pastor daddy and our family. We were leaving a city in the early morning without anyone seeing us off. I really didn't understand where we were moving or why. I only knew that my world was changing and no one had talked to me about anything that was happening.

I'm not trying to fault my parents. They would certainly have taken time to explain to me some of the situation if I had known to ask. However, many years down the road, I felt the same feelings in my present situation that I did then.

The next flash of understanding that came to my mind was a book I had recently read entitled, *The Transformation of the Inner Man* by John and Paula Sandford (Victory House). The chapter on Bitter Root Judgment and Expectancy had resonated in my heart and changed my life forward.

Suddenly I knew what was happening. I had bitterness and unforgiveness toward my father for being moved from place to place as a child without explanation. I had sown a judgment that all the men in my life would want to move me from place to place without explanation and I was reaping through my husband. I quickly repented for this sin, forgave my father, and broke the power of reaping through the power of Jesus' shed blood on the cross.

That night Mike came home from work and was whistling and happy. He didn't even mention selling the house. Later on that night I got the courage to ask him if he was still thinking about school. He smiled and said something like, "No, I thought about it again today and decided against going."

Defilement Through Bitter Roots

I went back and studied the Scriptures concerning bitter roots and sowing and reaping after that experience. Hebrews 12:15 says, "Looking carefully lest anyone fall short of the grace of God; lest any root of bitterness springing up cause trouble, and by this many become defiled." Amazing as it sounds, my bitterness had defiled Mike and caused big trouble for me!

The Sandfords have this to say about this defilement:

"Our bitter root, by the force of reaping, actually defiles others. We *make* them act around us in ways they might successfully resist, apart from us. Every married person or other kind of partner ought to ask, 'How come he didn't become a better and stronger person by associating with me?' And, 'Can it be that my bitter root is defiling him?' 'Am I reaping something through this person?'"[1]

Another biblical principle that fed into my situation was Galatians 6:7, "Do not be deceived, God is not mocked; for whatever a man sows, that he will also reap."

Not only do the seeds we sow come back to us, but they come back in a much greater measure than we have sown them. Hosea 8:7 says: "They sow to the wind and reap the whirlwind."

I had sown a judgment against my father and I reaped it through my husband! My father, the man in my life, had unknowingly caused me pain by not explaining the church situation and our subsequent leaving. Now, God was trying to reveal the bitterness that I had in that situation by allowing me to reap through my husband. Once the bitterness was revealed, the judgment repented for, and the power of unforgiveness broken, Mike was free to think for himself. My bitter root no longer defiled him.

Bitter roots often cause us to see situations through defiled lenses. When we judge someone's behavior and thus get bitter about it, our eye suddenly is clouded by what the Bible calls a plank. Matthew 7:1-5 says: "Judge not, that you be not judged. For with what judgment you judge, you will be judged, and with the measure you use, it will be measured back to you. And why do you look at the speck in your brother's eye, but do not consider the plank in your own eye? Or how can you say to your brother, 'Let me remove the speck from your eye'; and look, a plank in your own eye? Hypocrite! First remove the plank from your own eye and then you will see clearly to remove the speck from your brother's eye."

Bitter Root Judgments are Not the Same as Unforgiveness

We need to understand that making bitter root judgments is not the same as unforgiveness. The judgments that we make in bitterness actually start a cycle that will cause us to fall into the same set of situations over and over until we deal with the root issues in our lives. Our merciful, heavenly Father does this because sin, when it is full-grown, brings death (James 1:15).

The Lord Jesus died on the cross so we can experience life, and life more abundantly (John 10:10). Therefore, if there's anything in our life that goes against this, He wants to bring it to death on the cross.

When we judge another, we actually put a binding upon them and they cannot see their problems. They become im-

> The judgments that we make in bitterness actually start a cycle that will cause us to fall into the same set of situations over and over until we deal with the root issues in our lives. Our merciful, heavenly Father does this because sin, when it is full-grown, brings death.

prisoned in our judgment until we free them through releasing the judgment and forgiveness. Then we bring the power of the cross to bear on the situation and they are freed.

A really dramatic example of this came as a result of praying with a friend for her husband's salvation. During our prayer time she said with a mixture of disgust and sorrow, "George (not his real name) will never get born again! He doesn't even want to accept Christ." At that moment, the Holy Spirit quickened me to say, "Jewel (also not her real name), don't say that! You need to release him from that bitter root judgment so he can be free to receive the Lord into his life."

Jewel looked shocked for a moment, and then she realized what she had done. Right then, she prayed, "Father, I now repent for the judgment I have made of my husband, George, that he refuses to get born again and isn't even interested. In Jesus' Name. Amen." The next week her husband was born again.

Bitter root judgments are much more powerful than what counselors call "psychological expectancy." This occurs when people are hurt through authority figures and expect all other such leaders to treat them the same way. Actually, as we said earlier, the leaders are defiled and, even against their will, start to treat the person just like all other leaders in their past.

A side note on this is if we find ourselves acting uncharacteristically toward a certain person in our life, that person may be reaping through us. We may be fighting the defilement they are putting on us through their bitterness. It is possible to recognize this and break the defilement off ourselves. I have done this myself on more than one occasion. This really works, as I was able to treat the person quite differently after the prayer of release.

"Coals of Fire"

The Lord will bring us back to a certain situation when we first planted bitter roots and failed in our attitudes and judgments in order to ensure that we are healed of those root attitudes. In fact, even after we release those we judge, the Lord will often bring us into a similar situation to make sure that we have dealt with our pattern of thinking in that area. This has happened to me more than once in my life.

Even though I had released my judgments, forgiven the person, and broken the curse that comes through judging, my mind still needed to be renewed in that area. You might say that my soul needed to be restored (Psalm 23:3). For this reason, the Lord again brought me back into a similar situation where I was falsely judged through an authority figure, to bring healing into my life in that area.

This might be called a "coals of fire" experience. Do you remember the story where Jesus was on the shore and called to the disciples after His resurrection? (John 21:4-19). He asked them if they had any food. The key to this story is that He was cooking food for them by a coal fire—the same kind of fire that Peter stood by when he denied Christ. It was in this setting that the Lord said to Peter, "Simon, son of Jonah, do you love Me more than these?" He went on with a dissertation where Peter was told to feed His sheep and lambs, which ended with Jesus saying to Peter, "Follow me."

What a powerful picture of true forgiveness. The Lord brought Peter back to the place of his deepest, darkest shame, fed him, and commissioned Peter to follow Him. Essentially Jesus was saying, "Peter, I still love you and want you as My disciple. I forgive you."

This very kind of thing has happened to me concerning the church. Through the years I have been hurt by various male pastors who had promised to cover me. In the end, the relationships had contained both pain and blessings. However, for some, there was more pain than blessing.

When we moved to Colorado Springs and started going to church where our good friend, Dutch Sheets, was the pastor, I found myself struggling. I pinpointed the fact that Dutch had gone from my friend to an authority figure in my life. The glorious part of this story is that we are such good friends that I felt the freedom to tell him of my past hurt and old tapes that were playing in my head.

I'll never forget the day that he looked into my face and said, "Cindy, I'm going to prove all those other guys to be wrong in how they treated you. This is going to be a wonderful experience for you." You know what? He was right! Mike and I have greatly benefited from being at Springs Harvest Fellowship and Dutch has been a faithful covering and advocate when we have needed him.

It is critical in our Christian life to come to grips with the fact that old pain and bitterness produces defilement in our own hearts and lives. The Lord will be faithful to let us know the difference when our heart hurts and struggles arise within our souls, if we just ask Him to help us. The people in authority over us will bless us as well if we learn to discern the truth from old tapes of the past.

Releasing Bitter Root Judgments

The principle of releasing bitter root judgments is one of the most powerful truths I have learned in my own Christian walk. Anytime there is an unreasonable situation surrounding me, I always check to see if I have a root of bitterness.

Years ago I taught on this subject at a women's conference in the Dallas, Texas area. As I started to pray with people to release judgments against their family, a woman thought about her daughter. The daughter had disappeared a few years before and the family had not heard a word of her whereabouts

Releasing Bitter Root Judgments 33

since that time. Of course, this was a matter of deep distress for the whole family.

The lady released the judgments that she had made about her daughter. She released her from her judgment that her daughter was no good, and that she was a troublemaker. Another one was that her daughter didn't care how the family felt about her leaving. After we finished praying, we took a break. The woman was startled to receive a call from her long, lost daughter during that short break. The girl said to her mother, "Mom, I'm sorry that I left home. Can I come home?" Her mom replied through bountiful tears, "Oh honey, of course you can come home. Come home today!"

There are other stories which, while not so dramatic, are still quite meaningful. Mike and I had moved to El Paso, Texas and bought a big old home with a basement. The washer and dryer were in the basement and we had inherited them with the house. The dryer was a particular problem because it constantly overheated. I was quite afraid that the clothes might catch on fire; but with a small baby, I had mountains of dirty clothes to wash.

I told Mike the problem and asked him to look at it. (He is quite handy with fixing almost anything.) Alas, my appeals fell on deaf ears! From there I proceeded to nag, and then cry. The end of the process was me saying, "Mike Jacobs, you just don't care that our house might catch on fire and that I have piles of stinky clothes in the basement!"

After I calmed down the next day, I had a bolt of revelation that I had judged Mike for not wanting to ever help me around the house. The clothes dryer was just one of a long string of things in this regard. I quickly repented for my judgment and forgave Mike. That night he came home *without my asking* and fixed the dryer. Boy, was I ever excited – I simply danced around the house the next day in my devotional time! (I can't call it my quiet time, because I'm not always quiet in it.)

By now you might be thinking, "Okay, okay, Cindy, I give up! You have made your case. I know that I have lists and lists of judgments against my mother, father, brother, pastor, etc. Help me out here!"

I'm so glad you asked that because I am more than happy, as I am writing these words, to think that you are going to get really, really free in the next few moments.

Here's what you need to do:

1. Make a list of the relationships in your life that you might have formed judgments against. (Don't forget yourself!)

2. If possible, find a friend to pray with you to release them. James 5:16 says, "Confess your trespasses to one another, and pray for one another, that you may be healed. The effective, fervent prayer of a righteous man avails much."

3. If you do not have anyone to pray with you, don't worry, God is there for you and it is to Him that you are doing the confessing.

4. Ask the Holy Spirit to reveal to you any bitter roots that you are not aware of in your life.

5. Make a list of these judgments.

6. Begin to pray and release the person who has most hurt you or whom you are most reaping judgment through. It is usual to begin with the family of origin issues. Look for threads running through your life where there is a cycle of reaping (i.e., you are betrayed over and over, etc.)

7. Here is a sample prayer: "Father in the Name of Jesus Christ of Nazareth, I now release my judgments against my dad for the following things (list the judgments you have made against him. Some examples would be that he would never listen to me, that he was an angry man, etc.)."

    This is not to say that your dad was not angry, etc. or that you condone what he did, but you need to release him so the defilement you have will not affect any authority figures around you. It is also possible that there was some dishonor in the way you treated your parents and this will come back on you also. (Exodus 20:12 says, "Honor your father and your mother, that your days may be long upon the land which the Lord your God is giving you.")

8. Forgive those you have judged and ask the Lord to forgive you for judging.

9. Break the power of the reaping which has the effect of a curse upon your life. Say this, "I now break the curses that have been released against me as a result of my judging."

10. Apply the power of the cross into any area where you are reaping from the sowing of bitter root judgments in your life. A sample prayer would be, "Father God, I now bring the power of the cross to bear upon these bitter root judgments that I have made. I pray that their power will be broken today in my life."

I am very excited for you as you start a whole new beginning in your life from this day. The truth will set you and all those you love free as you walk in wholeness in Christ.

Notes
[1] John and Paula Sandford, *The Transformation of the Inner Man* (Tulsa, Okla.: Victory House, Inc., 1982), p. 263.

Chapter Three

Overcoming Rejection

Chris Hayward

Chris Hayward's call to ministry came in 1983 when he was ordained and served as associate pastor of a spirit-filled Baptist Church in Waco, Texas. After serving 10 years as a senior pastor, he became the Executive Director of Cleansing Stream Ministries. Chris is the author of *God's Cleansing Stream* and is on the faculty of Wagner Leadership Institute. He and his wife, Karen, were married in 1970 and have three children. To learn more about Cleansing Stream Ministries and available resources, please call 800-580-8190 or visit www.cleansingstream.org.

I know of no other act that can bring such pain as rejection. The spirit of rejection can be found in almost every novel or drama. It is ingrained in the very core of our being. Introduced in the Garden of Eden, it has continued to make its indelible mark on each of us. No one is exempt from the effects of rejection and only Jesus can deliver us from its death-producing results.

Some More Than Others

Though each of us can relate to the pain of rejection, there are some more than others, who have known its pain in greater measure. For example, to have been sexually molested by a family member would inflict a far greater sense of rejection than to have been fired from a job. However, the enemy of our souls will do whatever it takes to cause us to embrace the spirit of rejection. Later in this chapter you will understand just why the devil is so intent on inflicting this upon God's children.

Rejection in any form is painful. There are adults today whose lives are different because of a hurtful statement made by a teacher when they were in elementary
school. A child whose parent said to them, "You're stupid! I wish you'd never been born!" can be impacted for a
lifetime. Being the last one chosen to play on a team can
impact the thinking of a youngster and mold them toward
failure as an adult. These "little" rejections accumulate
over time and become like a mud slide rolling over everything in its path.

Defining The Term

The dictionary defines rejection as an act of "throwing away," or
"discarding" someone or something. Certainly that implies a
lack of value, which is precisely how we feel when rejected. We
begin to feel that we have no value. There comes an overwhelming sense of worthlessness. The dictionary defines rejection as
the act of "being denied love." Perhaps this is the most
significant explanation of all. Consequently, to the degree that
we embrace rejection, to that same degree there is a corresponding inability to give or receive love.

When we embrace the spirit of rejection we have difficulty
being able to fully receive the love of God. We might receive His
love intellectually, but find it awkward to experience it emotionally. This becomes equally true when others try to express love
toward us. Depending on the degree of rejection, we resist their
affections. Feeling worthless makes any attempt at affection seem
unreal. Correspondingly, we also find it hard to express love
toward God. Worship becomes an effort and intimacy with God
next to impossible. We also avoid getting too close to oth-

ers.   A polite distance is maintained as we find it very hard to trust.

The Spider's Web

One summer evening in Texas, I looked out my back door onto the deck.   There, under a light above the sliding door was a spider weaving his web.   As the evening wore on, I watched as it wove an intricate design with delicate precision.   By the time I went to bed it was complete.   I mused over the fact that in the morning I would take a broom and with one "swish" wipe away all signs of it being there.   I realized that this is precisely the way the devil works.   He might spend years weaving an intricate plan of rejection around our lives.   But with one sweep of the name of Jesus all traces can be removed.

You might think that the effects of rejection have been with you for so long you are doomed to despair for the rest of your life.   Be encouraged!   The power of Jesus' name can deliver you from its ugly entanglements.

"Behold, I give you the authority to trample on serpents and scorpions, and over all the power of the enemy, and nothing shall by any means hurt you" (Luke 10:19).

Satan's Strategy and God's Response

"The thief comes only to steal and kill and destroy; I have come that they may have life, and have it to the full" (John 10:10).

... to steal
The word for steal in Greek is *klepto*.   It is where we obtain the English word, kleptomaniac.   The manner by

which the enemy steals is by stealth – imperceptibly, without anyone noticing until it is too late. That which he wants to steal is our faith, our peace, our joy, and our liberation in Christ.

... and kill
The word used here is one that refers to "sacrifice." It is the intention of Satan that we would give ourselves over to worthless endeavors – that our lives would be void of purpose.

... and destroy
To destroy means to ruin. Our enemy would like nothing more than for us to look back at the end of our lives and see a worthless heap of rubble.

When Jesus said that He has come to bring us life to the full, it means that instead of taking away, He will add. Instead of our sacrificing ourselves to worthless things, He will give us purpose and destiny. And, rather than ruination, He will build something beautiful out of our lives.

Two Kingdoms

The Kingdom of Darkness
Based on John 10:10 and other verses, we know that Satan's kingdom is one where there is no love, no joy, no peace, no acceptance, and no forgiveness. There is only rejection, disillusionment, destruction, division, and despair. God is love. Satan hates God and therefore is opposed to everything that God is. But why would he want to "steal" the love of God out of our lives? In just a moment we'll see exactly why.

The Kingdom of God

God's kingdom is one of love, acceptance, and forgiveness. He offers us mercy and grace. He is the God of all hope. Inherent in the names of God are His attributes. He is the Shepherd who lays down His life for us (1 John 3:16). He is the Almighty One for whom nothing is too difficult (Psalm 46:7). He is our Healer who binds up our wounds (Exodus 15:26). He is The Righteousness One who makes us fit for Heaven (Jeremiah 33:16). He is our Peace who calms the troubled waters of our lives (Ephesians 2:14). Hc will never leave us or forsake us (Hebrews 13:5). And He is our Deliverer who has destroyed the works of darkness (Romans 11:26).

The Purpose of Rejection

There is no doubt that the very nature of our enemy is one of hatefulness toward God and humanity. God has placed His glory in us and has prepared for those who receive His Son an ultimate position even above the angels. Satan knows that he can rarely succeed in having us deny the Lord, or to give up our faith, so he has another way to make us ineffective. The following verse will show us how: "For in Jesus Christ neither circumcision availeth any thing, nor uncircumcision; but *faith which worketh by love"* (Gal. 5:6, KJV, emphasis mine).

The Scripture says quite clearly, "faith works through love." In other words, if we have great faith, it is because great love is behind it. If we have little faith, it is because there is little love at work in us. I have never seen someone who is exercising faith and doing great exploits for God who was also full of rejection. Remember, rejection is the act of being denied love. Those who are subject to the spirit of rejection are too worried about what others think of them. They become so self-centered that they cannot function in faith. This is why Satan's plan works so well. He knows we won't deny the Lord, so he works stealthily as the kleptomaniac and gradually steals our love for God and others – our joy of serving Him, and the peace of His presence – filling us with rejection. Through time, and given enough incidents of rejection and pain by others toward us, he gradually steals the love of God from our heart. We then end up with a church that is full of rejection. Hence splits and divisions come within the Body of Christ. The church becomes anemic and ineffective. The enemy has accomplished what he set out to do – in essence he gets us to become a "faith-less" people.

Over time certain walls are erected around the hearts of people. We have found that behind each wall there is a demonic assignment to perpetuate and maintain that particular wall of rejection.

The Four Walls of Rejection

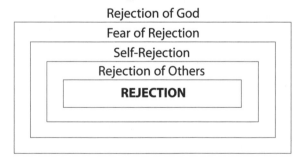

Rejection of God
Fear of Rejection
Self-Rejection
Rejection of Others
REJECTION

Walls come in many forms. There are physical walls and there are emotional walls. Though not named in the Bible as such, we can clearly see their effects in the lives of many throughout Scripture. In particular we look at Adam and Eve. Behind each wall a demonic attack is waged to perpetuate rejection. The enemy works through deception. For him to be effective we must buy in to his deception, reject God's truth, and embrace a lie. Therefore we must repent wherever we have given in and failed to trust God. Then we must renounce every place of agreement with the devil's lies. Finally, we break the yoke of bondage to which we have submitted. Included in this chapter are prayers that I would encourage you to pray from your heart. It is God's desire that you would be set free from the spirit of rejection.

The Rejection of God

"So when the woman saw that the tree was good for food, that it was pleasant to the eyes, and a tree desirable to make one wise, she took of its fruit and ate. She also gave to her husband with her, and he ate" (Genesis 3:6).

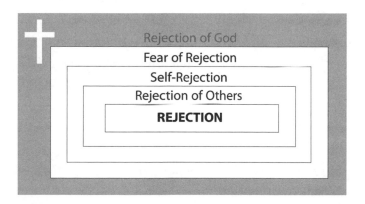

This first wall is what I call a "load-bearing" wall. Without it the others cannot be erected. If it goes up, the others are sure to follow. Most of us are more concerned about our own rejection and fail to come to grips with the fact that in many ways we have rejected God. We have rejected His Word, His ways, His character, and His love.

Eve was deceived into believing that God no longer cared about her best interests. Perhaps she believed that He had rejected her. The dialogue in the Garden is quite clear that the serpent was attempting to place God in a bad light – questioning His motives, etc. She was finally convinced that she needed to take matters into her own hands. She rejected God and ate from the forbidden tree. Adam, standing beside her did the same. "...she took of the fruit thereof, and did eat, and gave also unto her husband with her; and he did eat" (Gen. 3:6).

We become impatient with God. Why won't He answer our prayers? Why won't He change this or that situation? When will He come through for us? Why is He restricting us? Then we, like Adam and Eve, take matters into our own hands, rejecting God's love, God's Word, and God's ways. The wall of rejecting God goes up, and is built, making room for others. As we approach these walls I would invite you to repent of any place you have allowed them to surround you, renouncing the enemy and breaking his stronghold over your life.

Prayer

Father God, I repent of rejecting You and Your Word. Forgive me, Lord, for not believing that You love and accept me. I repent of taking things into my own hands. I repent of my pride, stubbornness, self-will, and rebellion. I renounce and reject all rejection of God and the spirit behind it. I refuse to accept its influence in my life any longer. I break every word, and all agreements I have made with the spirit of rejection of God. I break all connections and generational influences that have to do with the spirit of rejection of God. And now, because of what Jesus has done on the cross, and the authority He has given to me, I come against the wall of rejection of God and break it down in Jesus' name!

The Fear of Rejection

"And they heard the sound of the LORD God walking in the garden in the cool of the day, and Adam and his wife hid themselves from the presence of the LORD God among the trees of the garden" (Genesis 3:8).

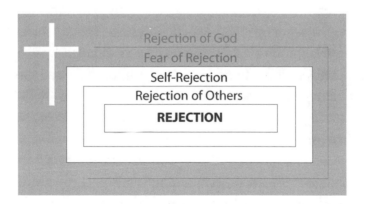

Once we have opened the door to rejection by rejecting God, it is only a matter of time before other walls are erected. One such wall is the fear of rejection. Adam and Eve "hid themselves" from God. They were fearful of God's response to their act of rebellion. They had never feared before. Sin warps our perception of God. We begin to credit Him with sinful motivations because we now see Him through the eyes of rejection. This is why it is so important that our mind be renewed through the washing of God's Word (Romans 12:12). The debris must be washed away. We must take on the mind of Christ.

Just as Adam and Eve hid themselves, we also hide ourselves through the fear of rejection. We begin to distrust God and others. We are suspicious of people's intentions. We enter into temporary relationships. Have you ever noticed how some people purposely sabotage relationships? You seem to be getting close to someone, and then suddenly they pull away.

When we are being oppressed with self-rejection, we sometimes reject others before they have an opportunity to reject us out of fear. We say, "No one is ever going to hurt me like that again. I will put up a wall and hide from the pain of potentially hurtful relationships." In doing this we continue to feed rejection. Our greatest fears have come upon us – and this has brought more rejection.

Prayer

Father, I repent of all deception and lying, suspicion, mistrust, control, and manipulation. I repent of trying to please people instead of seeking to please You. I renounce the spirit behind the fear of rejection. I reject its lies. I break all words or agreements with the fear of rejection. I break all connections and generational influences with the fear of rejection. *Fear of rejection, in the name of Jesus, I come against you and break down your wall.*

Self-Rejection

"Then the eyes of both of them were opened, and they knew that they were naked; and they sewed fig leaves together and made themselves coverings" (Genesis 3:7).

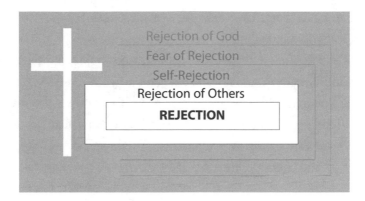

It doesn't take a botanist to realize that fig leaves soon wither and die. They are temporary at best. How overwhelming is the love of God! Have you noticed that God sought out Adam and Eve? It is natural that we feel shame for the sinful things we have done. It was never God's intention that we "cover" ourselves with shame. Jesus died and rose again to take upon Himself our sin and our "shame."

Many hurtful things come from this form of self-rejection. Everything from eating disorders to low self-esteem and suicide are rooted in this malicious spirit. God didn't demand that they appear before Him in a tribunal; instead He sought them out. It was then that the Lord replaced their coverings of shame for something redemptive. For the first time an animal was slain. Its blood was shed and its skin became a covering for Adam and Eve.

"Also for Adam and his wife the LORD God made tu-
nics of skin, and clothed them" (Genesis 3:21).

God does this with us also. When we feel our lives are
worthless, hopeless – when all thoughts of drawing close to
God seem shattered, He shows up. We can be certain that He
will not relent until we discard worthlessness for the eternal.
His love demands that.

Dear brother and sister – you can't be replaced! There is
no soul like yours, and no one else can be you! And God trea-
sures you and who you are. How beautifully this is portrayed
by what happened on the cross. His blood was shed for us to
cover sin and shame for each of us. We have been clothed in
Christ – the Eternal One – the Redeemer!

Prayer

Father, I repent of rejecting myself. I repent of hat-
ing your creation. I repent of resisting Your plan
for my life. I repent of trying to be someone I
was never meant to be. I repent of always needing
the approval of others. I choose to accept Your love
for me and what I am meant to be. Spirit of self-
rejection I renounce you. I break your power. I
break your authority. I break every curse and vow
that has given you room to operate in my life. I
choose to accept God's Word, God's love, and
God's ways for my life. Lord, break the stronghold of self-rejection off my life now, I ask in Jesus
name.

The Rejection of Others

"Then the man said, 'The woman whom You gave to be with me, she gave me of the tree, and I ate.' And the LORD God said to the woman, 'What is this you have done?' The woman said, 'The serpent deceived me, and I ate'" (Genesis 3:12-13).

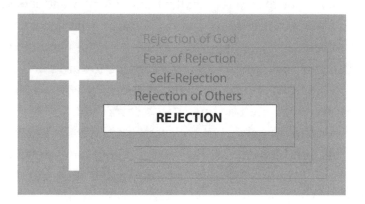

When we don't want to accept personal responsibility for our own actions we look for opportunities to blame others. We put up walls – first against God, and then very quickly it moves to others and ourselves. We begin to look for someone or something to blame. A husband blames his wife and the wife her husband for not meeting their expectations. We say, "If she had only been more supportive," or "If he had only been more loving and caring." Racial hatred and bigotry all find themselves under the control of the spirit of rejecting others. We must choose to be a loving and forgiving people. If not, we are bound and tormented – imprisoned by the spirit of rejection.

"And his lord was wroth, and delivered him to the tormentors, till he should pay all that was due unto him. So likewise shall my heavenly Father do also unto you, if ye from your hearts forgive not every one his brother their trespasses" (Matthew 18:34-35, KJV).

I invite you to come before the Lord right now and choose to forgive the ones that have grievously brought pain into your life. Some feel they cannot forgive because they still nurse the pain and hurt. You don't have to feel all loving toward someone to forgive them. It is a choice – not a feeling. When you choose to forgive, you are obeying God's command.

"For if you forgive men their trespasses, your heavenly Father will also forgive you. But if you do not forgive men their trespasses, neither will your Father forgive your trespasses" (Matthew 6:14-15).

The feelings may or may not come later on, but our freedom will come immediately. To forgive does not mean to excuse. What they did to hurt you might have been inexcusable and wicked. Release them and be released. Let God be their judge.

Prayer

Father, I repent of rejecting others. I repent for being unforgiving, resentful, and bitter toward others. I repent for allowing the hurt that I received to move me to reject others before they could reject me. Spirit of rejection of others, I renounce you. I refuse to accept your influence in my life any longer. I choose to be a person of acceptance not rejection. I break all words, agreements and connections with you. I break all generational influences that would give strength to the rejection of others.

Now, Spirit of rejection, your stronghold has been dismantled, you have no protection. I come against you and I reject you. Your defeat was accomplished at the cross of Jesus. I tell you that your rule in my life ends here, now! Because of the Spirit of God, who gives me power and authority, I command you to loose me from your hold. I command you to leave me now in Jesus' name.

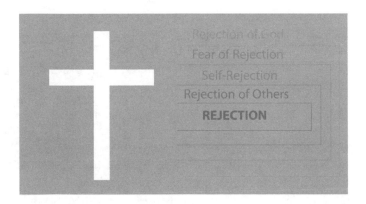

The Lord wants His Church to be strong, vibrant, and healthy. The Body of Christ is as healthy as its individual members. For us to be a people that move in great faith, we must be a people who also move in the power of God's love. Rejection must go – it is an enemy of God and a destroyer of God's people. May we all grow in the love and grace of the Lord, Jesus Christ. Amen.

Chapter Four

Deliverance from Fear and Anger

John L. Sandford

John Sandford and his wife, Paula, are cofounders of Elijah House, an international ministry which seeks to spread the word of restoration and reconciliation through prayer counseling ministry, teaching and equipping, and providing audio, video, and written materials for use in home fellowships, Christian adult education, and for personal and family ministry. The Sandfords' books are well known and used around the world and include *Healing the Wounded Spirit* and *A Comprehensive Guide to Deliverance and Inner Healing* as well as other numerous titles. For more information on the Elijah House or available resources, please contact them at S. 1000 Richards Road, Post Falls, ID 83854 or call 208-773-1645.

There is an enemy. Normally, we as Christians are protected (Psalm 91:11). We are hidden in Christ (Colossians 3:3). But sins expose us, and the uncrucified aspects of our sin nature offer theatres of operation and control to demonic forces.

Inherited Oppression

But demons can access us through other avenues in addition to our own sins or sin nature. I once ministered to a man whose mother was a prostitute and continued her trade until she grew too large to attract customers. Because of her sin, he came out of the womb already inhabited by demons of lust.

Sometimes it is the sins of our ancestors that have invited demonic oppression into our lives. Many innocent people have been afflicted because a forefather or mother was active in Masonry or Eastern Star, or some other form of magic or witchcraft (see Deuteronomy 5:9 and 18:9-13).

If you are struggling with this kind of issue, or are ministering to someone who is, be assured that inherited demonic oppression is often relatively easy to deliver. You simply help the person to repent for their own sins and those of their forbearers, and then cast away whatever demons may have found lodging because of it. It will be necessary for the person to renounce the occult and then close all the doors of their heart and mind; remove the open invitations. But if they do that, freedom usually persists.

Oppression Through Practiced Emotional Habit

It is a different matter to be set free from emotional constructs in our own character (habits of feeling and reacting, or "practices," see Colossians 3:9-10). These are more internal than anything we may have inherited. They are practiced ways of responding that we have woven more or less integrally into the very fiber of our character. In the instances cited above, once we have seen the origin of demonization through the sins of others or by inheritance, the battle is largely won. Repentance and authority easily dislodge the demonic. But when a demon has inhabited a practiced emotional habit in our character, much more than simple deliverance will be required if the demon is to be prevented from returning with other demons seven times worse (Luke 11:26).

Satan is not present everywhere nor is he omniscient (knowing everything). Consequently, a person may develop a character flaw, a fearful way, or a habit of anger for quite a while before a demon finds that open door. This is not so when a person enters into occult activities. Magic is the home field of the demonic, and instant demonization occurs. But it may be quite a while before demons take up residence in that emotionally sinful "home" in us.

Infestation

When demons do find room in us, then there are several levels of demonization that can occur. The first is *infestation*. Picture a person's head surrounded by buzzing hornets. Demons may be all around, but not yet *in* the person. Whenever he or she falls into acting out a habit of fear or anger (or any other negative emotion), an encircling demon has access to reach in and temporarily increase or even control through that emotion – which then becomes a panic attack or a tantrum (or lust or whatever). But when the person "comes to themself," throws off whatever they were feeling, repents of what they were doing, and is forgiven, demonic influence is snapped off. The person was not inhabited, only demonized. That door can be kept from re-opening when the person sees their habitual fleshly way, repents of it and, best yet, discovers how that originated in their life, prays for forgiveness, forgives others, and carries that practice to death on the cross.

Inhabitation

The second level is *inhabitation*. In such cases, there is a degree of demonic entrance and struggle. But one ought not to speak of it as possession, rather as being demonized. A demon has only been allowed to inhabit exterior portions of the mind and character. Nevertheless, warfare is on because the Holy Spirit will not allow anything demonic to remain uncontested in the person so near to His own domicile in the heart. The Christian may quickly cast out or encyst (encapsulate) the demon, like a tubercular infection surrounded by white cells, keeping it encased and ineffectual.

That was my case. Dabbling in occult researches before I came to Christ, as well as entertaining a long practiced and hidden emotion of fear, I had allowed a demon to gain access. But the prayers of those around me, and my own strength of character, had forbidden the demon any theatre of operation and had imprisoned it. Shortly after I was born anew and Holy Spirit-filled, that demon was forced to the surface. Friends cast it away, I repented of occultism, renounced it, closed all the doors and was free.

Obsession

The third level is *obsession*. This is both a spiritual and psychological condition. A demon has found access to the mind and character, and has been allowed to increase its influence and dominion. Almost always, it has invited other demons to help in the warfare to control the person. So, in cases of obsession, seldom are we dealing with only one demon. This was the case for Mary Magdalene, from whom the Lord cast out seven demons (Mark 16:9). Part of the time an obsessed Christian is freed from demonic control, able to be who God intended. At other times, when something stimulates, there is a dramatic switch, and the person is once again under the control of the demonic. Secular psychologists, seeing that behavior, unaware of the demonic, have labeled such people "obsessive-compulsive." Insofar as that describes the condition and activity of our flesh, it's probably a fitting diagnosis. But what that term actually describes is the return of the character flaws through which demons can manipulate and increasingly control the person.

In cases of obsession, deliverance cannot be effected merely by naming the condition – fear, hatred, anger, lust, etc., as though the demonic specialists of those emotions were all that is involved. Please understand: fear and anger are not initially demons. They are usually practiced habits in our flesh. We are not to cast out flesh. Flesh is to be taken to the cross by confession, repentance, forgiveness and "reckoning as dead on the cross" (see Romans 6:11).

When Christians continue to practice a forbidden habit (fear, anger, etc.), it becomes obsessive. At some point in the process of development, a demon finds that habit to be an available "home," and invites others in. Demons specialize. So if the house is "anger," a demon of anger enters, molds itself to the habit of getting angry and has every opportunity to expand the reactions, throwing the perpetrator/victim into ever-accelerating tantrums.

A demon of fear may indwell the habit of fear and throw the person into panic attacks; however, you should note that not all panic attacks are demonic or demonically induced. In any case, they are always open invitations for demons to come and increase their impact and frequency. Sometimes, a demon must first be cast away before you can lead the person into recognition of the habit, offering repentance for it, forgiveness for those who caused it, and death of the habit through the cross.

Sometimes the Lord guides you differently, and before you can successfully cast away the controlling demon, you must dismantle his house. It is important to understand that deliverance ministry is always a matter of following the Holy Spirit's guidance. It is never a set of hard and fast rules and incantations that work every time. Therefore,

> It is important to understand that deliverance ministry is always a matter of following the Holy Spirit's guidance. It is never a set of hard and fast rules and incantations that work every time. Therefore, there are no formulas guaranteed to work, like recipes for baking. ...We must follow the fresh guidance of the Holy Spirit each time.

there are no formulas guaranteed to work, like recipes for baking. *Whenever we are dealing with emotional constructs and the demons that influence or inhabit them, we need to deal with both the demonic and the natural, and we must follow the fresh guidance of the Holy Spirit each time.*

We may cast away the demonic and then heal the house, or we may dismantle the house by healing the personality and character and then do away with the demonic. Since the casting and the dismantling are done in the power of the Holy Spirit, whichever must be done first will be dictated by the Holy Spirit's unique guidance in each instance. Paula and I usually find ourselves dismantling the devil's abode first, but not always.

Possession

The fourth level is *possession.* Possession means that demons have gained full control. The original personality is totally suppressed; what remains to speak and be in control is the devil's henchman. Possession is rare. I have never seen a Christian possessed, though I have seen full possession of non-Christians in pagan countries. *I do not believe full possession can happen to born-anew Christians.* He Who is in us is stronger than he who is in the world, and He will not allow it. In this I agree with the many who say a Christian cannot be possessed. But I also know Christians can be demonized on the other three levels, because I have ministered to hundreds of cases in each level.

The Fruit of the Flesh

We were not created to be hateful, or fearful, or filled with lust, envy, malice, or any other of the dire fruits of the flesh. God created us in His image to manifest all the fruits of His Holy Spirit. So the first cause of fear or anger lies in original sin. *Though succumbing to fear or anger (or any other fruit of the flesh) is abnormal, far from who we really are, ever since the Fall it has become normal behavior to struggle with all the fruits of the flesh.* It becomes abnormal and then provides a house for the demonic whenever we, as Christians, postpone repentance and aversion, or refuse to take the Christian actions we should – of prayer, forgiveness, mercy, loving actions, and so on.

Fear

Paul wrote, "For God has not given us a spirit of timidity [fear], but of power and love and discipline [other versions say `a sound mind']" (2 Timothy 1:7); and "Be angry, and yet do not sin; do not let the sun go down on your anger, and do not give the devil an opportunity" (Ephesians 4:6). Some Christians think that to be afraid is a sin, continually confessing their fears as though they had broken some eternal laws. But fear is a normal and healthy reaction built into us by God the Creator. If we knew no fear, we would not leap out of the way of a speeding car. Or, we might step off a building twenty floors up. Or we might foolishly stand in the line of fire in battle. Fear is good. It is what we do with fear that makes it either good or unhealthy, obsessive if unchecked, and finally demonized.

Anger

The same is true for anger. Anger is healthy. It is a mark of our love for one who is misbehaving, or our concern for justice, or a reaction to unjust wounding, etc. We do not need to be continually repenting and asking forgiveness for getting angry. Being angry is not sinful. Our Lord never sinned. But the Scripture says that Jesus, "...after *looking around at them with anger,* grieved at their hardness of heart..." healed the man with the withered hand, on the Sabbath day (Mark 3:5, emphasis mine). Anger is one of the Lord's watchmen for our heart, informing us when actions need to be taken. For Christians, anger is a call to ministry, for understanding, for forgiveness and possible reconciliation. Unfortunately, even among Christians, anger has too often been something to use – to dominate, manipulate, control, or just bluff people away for self-centered protection. Again, it is what we do with this anger that makes us either Christ-like or sinful; that invites either the flow of the Holy Spirit or begs demonic help.

The Problem with Suppression

When we don't admit we have fear or anger and suppress them, that does untold damage inside our hearts. When suppression becomes a habit – for instance, a false or foolish effort to maintain self-control (rather than release the emotion through prayer and understanding) – that begins the construction of a practiced habit which invites demonic access.

Suppression would seem to be the opposite of constantly unleashing fear or anger and thus building a habit of uncontrolled panic or rage. But, in actual fact, both invite the demonic. The difference is that because fear and anger are suppressed, the person most often doesn't think he has either; whereas they are fomenting like a volcano inside, and will someday erupt into a panic attack or a tantrum.

Dead to Self and Alive to Him

Whichever is the case, what is really needed is to ferret out, by discussion and listening with the ears of the Holy Spirit, what are the origins of fear and anger in the person's life. It will not do simply to perceive demonic operation and command the devil away. As we have said before, both deliverance and healing are needed. Counsel and prayer can heal and deliver and set the person free from recurrences. It is a joyous and fulfilling ministry to be a servant for the Lord, to bring His comfort and freedom to troubled souls. But demons and deliverance are not what is important, however exciting that ministry may become. Nor is inner healing foremost in importance, however satisfying and fulfilling to do or to receive. What, or Who, is important is the Lord, and obedience to Him.

Whoever would be of service to the Lord and to others in any ministry, but especially in the heart-touching ministries of deliverance and healing, must avoid allowing himself or herself to get carried away in the ministry by running wholly on experience or psychic gifting. *We are called every day, in each moment of ministry, to die to what we know and are, in order to be a tool of precision in the hand of the Lord.* It is the Lord Who is important, and His Kingdom. It is to Him all glory belongs. In other words, the more successful and power-filled the ministries of deliverance and healing become, the more assiduously we must take care to humble ourselves, remind ourselves of our sinful mortality, and return all glory to the Lord.

For example, if on a given day, the Holy Spirit reveals a root cause of fear or anger in the first person who comes to me for ministry, guess what will happen if I do not immediately put that revelation on the altar and die to it? That's what the next several counselees will have, whether they actually have it or not. I'm "into that" today. Ministry to people afflicted naturally and/or demonically by fear and anger demands not so much that we know a lot of stuff, but that we are dead to self and alive to Him each day.

Fear and Anger
in the Deliverance Minister

What are the two things that more than anything else keep us enmeshed in self rather than ministry to others?   Fear and anger!   We each have our own fears – that we won't do it right, that this time we'll fail.   So we lose trust of the freshness of the Holy Spirit's insights and turn back to rely on what we know or think we can do by experience.

We need to continually be aware that anger builds even within us, based on perceived failures or temporary deliverances.   For example, God may not yet have delivered someone we have prayed for, or a person may seem unable to take hold for themselves, and may keep coming back refilled with fear and anger still begging for deliverance. You name it.   It's your problem.

What I am saying is as old as Jesus telling us that, if we would take a splinter out of our brother's eye, we had better first take the log out of our own.   Whoever enters upon the battlefield of deliverance and healing ministry will find themself skewered by the Lord's lance more often than they defeat the devil or pierce anyone else's heart with insights and truth.   If they do not find it so, either they aren't listening, or something is causing them stubbornly to head for their own demonic enmeshment and need for deliverance. How many ministers of the Lord have we seen fall by the wayside?

Fear and anger beset ministering Christians every day, perhaps more than the people God sends to be delivered and
healed! This means that each of use who would set others
free will have to maintain a lively fellowship with God. It is
only His perfect love that casts out fear and enables us to
continue fresh and joyful in Him, while He uses us to scour
the debris of fear and anger from others.

The Good News

The good news is manifold: That God wants and is able to
deliver and heal His children of fear and anger and every
other emotional problem and demonic thing. That He is
still foolishly loving enough to keep on delivering and healing us foolish people who keep on getting into unnecessary
scrapes. That He risks the glory of His ministry through us
frail vessels – again and again. That the battle is already
won, and we have the strength-creating job of a mop-up
ministry. That He Who could do it all by a snap of His
fingers still lets us have the joy of delivering and healing
alongside our wonderful Lord. That we are equipped with
power and authority to cast away every kind of demon. And
that, in the end, we will have worked ourselves out of a
job, because someday nobody will ever again need to be
delivered and healed of fear and anger – or any other lousy
thing! Praise the Lord, and hallelujah!

Chapter Five

How Trauma Affects the Whole Person

Peter Horrobin

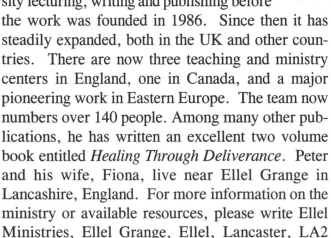

Peter Horrobin is the International Director of Ellel Ministries. After graduating at Oxford, he spent many years in University lecturing, writing and publishing before the work was founded in 1986. Since then it has steadily expanded, both in the UK and other countries. There are now three teaching and ministry centers in England, one in Canada, and a major pioneering work in Eastern Europe. The team now numbers over 140 people. Among many other publications, he has written an excellent two volume book entitled *Healing Through Deliverance*. Peter and his wife, Fiona, live near Ellel Grange in Lancashire, England. For more information on the ministry or available resources, please write Ellel Ministries, Ellel Grange, Ellel, Lancaster, LA2 0HN, England or visit www.ellel.org.

Trauma is a side-effect of events that happen to us which are beyond our control. A traumatic event can be anything from a road accident or falling down stairs to sexual abuse or the sudden receipt of bad news. None of us can ever plan for such events and by their very nature we are always unprepared for them.

There can be both short-term and long-term consequences of traumatic events. How we are affected by them can depend on a wide range of factors including: the severity of the incident, the local circumstances, who was involved and our attitude toward them, our own temperament, our physical fitness and resilience, our emotional well-being, our upbringing, our age, our former experiences, and our spirituality and personal wholeness in Christ.

An incident which may have been very traumatic for one person, could prove to be of little consequence to another. Two people of the same age may fall down the same flight of stairs and suffer identical physical injuries. The one who slipped and fell because they were carrying too much is less likely to carry trauma into later life than the one who slipped and fell because they were trying to escape the attentions of an abusive father. Two boys may fall off a boat into shallow water. The six-foot teenager may finish up sitting in the water laughing at his predicament, but the five-year old may be beneath the surface, face down in mud, inhaling water and fighting for his life. Years later the teenager may not even have a memory of the incident, whereas the five-year old may as an adult have a chronic fear of water, never learn to swim, suffer regular panic attacks, and finish up with breathing problems all his life.

Where We Suffer Trauma

Medically speaking, a trauma is the physical damage that is incurred by an organ of the body through an injury. I took my son tenpin bowling and was careless enough to drop a bowling ball on my foot. When I limped into Accident and Emergency at 1:00 am in the morning the nurse on duty wrote on her admission form, *"Trauma to the left big toe."* I tried to correct her by saying, *"No, my big toe is broken, the only trauma I experienced was through having done something so stupid in front of my son!"*

But technically the nurse was right. It is the part that is affected by the injury which suffers the trauma. But that statement invites a much wider question. How can we be so sure that when we have a physical injury, the consequences are limited to the physical realm and that other parts of our being are not also affected by the injury and, therefore, traumatized?

Mothers instinctively know the answer to this very basic, but important question. A three-year old may suffer one of the hundreds of minor injuries that are part of life's rich learning experience! In the rough and tumble of play, the child falls over and bangs their forehead on some concrete. The child instantly bursts into tears and runs to Mummy. Mummy opens her arms wide, takes the child onto her lap and *"kisses it better!"*

There is absolutely nothing physically therapeutic in that kiss, but its effect is usually instant and dramatic. The kiss does not speed up the rate of physical healing, but the love and the security of mother's love almost instantly removes the trauma from their hurting child's inner being! If Mother pushed the child away and refused to show care and love to such a young child in their moment of need, then the crying would go on much longer and the inner trauma would be at the root of an unhealed memory.

All Parts Are Involved

God created us with spirit, soul, and body. In 1 Thessalonians 5:23, Paul expresses concern that his readers should be whole in all three areas. While we may use the words "spirit, soul, and body" to describe three distinct and different aspects of what God created when he made man, in reality whatever happens to one part affects the others. During life they are indissolubly joined. It is only at death that the body is separated from the rest of our being.

It is impossible for one part of our humanity to experience anything which the other parts are not also involved in or affected by. A person may train their body to be supremely fit and win a gold medal at the Olympic Games. When the medals are handed out, the neck of the body may be used to hang the medal on, but the person whose body has run the race receives the praise. No athlete would say, *"Oh, don't praise me, it's my body that did it!"* The medal was actually won by a remarkable team effort of spirit, soul, and body!

If we, as God's creation, therefore, are so much joined together as spirit, soul, and body, cannot the spirit and soul also suffer the consequences of physical trauma? And cannot the body begin to suffer when trauma of a different nature affects the soul? Without doubt the answer to these very important questions is a resounding "Yes!"

It was when we first realized, for example, the extent of damage there can be to the inner self (spirit and soul – especially the emotions), through injury or suffering of the outer self (body), that God taught us an incredibly profound healing principle. Through prayerful application of this principle, we have seen a great deal of physical healing take place – often from the consequences of events that took place many years earlier.

The medical profession is intricately and correctly trained to treat the traumas that affect the body. After an accident, it is their immediate responsibility to take emergency action to save and preserve life, followed by restorative treatment. But what are the further consequences of these traumas if the inner being is not treated with the same care and attention to detail as the medics give to the body? The effects can range from lifelong fears through emotional instability, suicidal tendencies, and physical disability.

Lynda's Story

Lynda was a young woman who suffered from all of these symptoms. Life had become intolerable for her and she had lost hope. When we first met Lynda, she was 26 years of age, registered disabled with the Australian Government, receiving a lifetime disability pension. She was in constant pain, suffering severe side-effects of her medications, very depressed, and suicidal. When asked if we could pray for her, she initially refused. She had been prayed for so many times already without effect, that she did not want to run the risk of finding out once more that God didn't answer prayer.

She told us her story of how three years previously she had been mountain walking at night with her church youth group. No one had warned her of the dangers of the particular path they were on. She took a step off the pathway and fell off the edge of a cliff into a ravine, falling 35 feet through open space before landing on the rocks below. Her back was broken in four places and it was ten and a half hours before she was lifted out on a stretcher by helicopter. What a trauma! The doctors did everything they could possibly have done at the time, and also in the subsequent years. But three years later nothing more could be done for her medically. Her only option was to try and live with the consequences of her accident for the rest of her days.

Gently we began to explain to Lynda that when we suffer physical injury, we are also injured on the inside. Her body had been broken by the fall, but whatever had happened to her body had also happened to her spirit and soul. We told her a few stories of how others had been healed physically when God had brought healing on the inside. We explained how the body (the outer self) is often a reflector of what is happening on the inside (the inner self), and that it is sometimes impossible for the body to be fully healed until the person on the inside has also been healed.

We shared with her from the Scriptures how Isaiah prophesied that one of the ministries of Jesus would be the *"healing of the brokenhearted."* When she understood that the word for broken used here in Isaiah 61:1 actually means *"shattered into separate pieces"* and that not only had her body been broken by the fall, but that her heart (her spirit and soul, her inner being) had also been shattered, she began to understand what must have happened to her in the accident.

The Light of Hope; The Healing of Trauma

Slowly the light of hope began to dawn in her eyes and she came to a place where she was not only willing to be prayed for once more, but willing also to let others share in what God was doing, so that they could learn at the same time. We had met Lynda at a special conference for Christian medics. She was there because she had been a nurse. When it came to the time of prayer, therefore, she was surrounded by dozens of medical workers ranging from anaesthetists to pain consultants, from surgeons to physiotherapists!

They all watched as God worked a miracle in her body before their very eyes, and healed her of the trauma which was locked on the inside. We asked God to expose the pain which lay in Lynda's broken heart. She instantly fell to the ground, lying in the position she had been in when she fell off the cliff. It was as if part of her inner being was still lying at the foot of the cliff – shattered, traumatized, but unnoticed and, therefore, unhealed. We spoke love and gentleness into her spirit and soul. We asked Jesus to begin to heal her on the inside. We took her through forgiveness of those who should have warned her of the danger.

Whenever people go through severe trauma, there is a danger that their extreme vulnerability at the time will be used by the enemy to hold them under demonic control. This had happened in Lynda's case – she was gripped by fear on the inside. We delivered her of the spirits of fear and infirmity that had taken advantage of her traumatized state. We also had to deliver her of things which had taken advantage of subsequent traumas she experienced through sometimes frightening hospital treatments.

When we had prayed everything the Lord led us to pray, we then blessed some oil and anointed her for physical healing. With all those medics we watched in amazement as God poured his Holy Spirit into her and we saw her broken body being put back together by the hand of God. The body is normally a natural self-healer, but Lynda's body had been prevented from being healed by all the consequences of trauma that had been locked on the inside at the time of her injuries.

Five Years Later

Shortly after this Lynda caused consternation in the Sydney pensions benefits office. Never before had they had someone who had been affirmed (by three separate doctors) as being disabled for life, then ask to come off her pension because she was healed! Five years later Lynda fulfilled what was previously an impossible dream. She found God's man for her life, got married and is now looking forward to having a family!

God truly is a worker of miracles. But as we pray for people, it is important that we also do our part in bringing healing to them. So often when a person is suffering physically, people only pray for the healing of the body. But when the condition has origins which are related to traumatic events, then it is important to pray for the broken heart and not just for the broken body. The body cannot be fully healed while it is still reflecting the inner pain of the unhealed trauma.

The Need for Deliverance

When praying for people who have been traumatized, it is also essential to have a right understanding of the possible need for deliverance. Satan is no respecter of persons and he will use every possible opportunity to gain access to a person's life through the demonic, no matter who they are. The more traumatic the event the more vulnerable a person is.

Those incidents that carry with them the worst traumas to the inner self are usually those which have been done deliberately by someone who should have been in a position of spiritual covering and protection. When parents, close relations, teachers, ministers, and others whom a child would naturally want to trust, are the source of the abusive trauma, then the consequent damage and related demonic influence is always greater.

In the area of sexual abuse, the inner trauma is sometimes only exposed when a person gets married. Painful memories, raw emotions and the demonic can all be brought to the surface through the expectation of sexual fulfillment. Physical sexual relations can then become a time of intense fear and

---

The body cannot be fully healed while it is still reflecting the inner pain of the unhealed trauma.

---

panic. Instead of being a source of joy and fulfillment, they are destructive of the very relationship that the victim most desires. This also needs to be a part of the healing process.

In a short chapter like this it is not possible to go into greater detail about how to bring healing to those who have been damaged through abuse, but the principles of healing the consequences of trauma, whether the trauma is caused by an innocent accident or by deliberate abuse, are fundamentally the same.

"How Long?"

When Jesus brought healing to the epileptic boy, he asked his father, *"How long has he been like this?"* (Mark 9:21). That is an important question, since the answer can lead us to understand how to pray for the right thing. Perhaps the largest single reason why people are not healed is often because the wrong thing is being prayed for!

A lady came for prayer wearing a neck brace and asked for prayer for her asthma. It was tempting to anoint her with oil and pray for physical healing, but God prompted me to ask the Jesus question! "Thirty-three years" was her instant answer! "How old are you," I asked. "Thirty six." "So what happened when you were three years old?" I responded. "I was in a small plane landing on an Indonesian island. The plane crashed. Everyone else was killed, but because I was a child I had been strapped into a seat and survived."

Immediately I knew what to pray for. I asked God to bring healing to the terrified child on the inside – the child whose chest had been crushed by the seat harness as the plane had hit the ground, and the child whose neck had been thrown forward at the moment of impact. It was as if that broken-hearted and traumatized child was still lying in the remains of the plane on that remote island.

We spoke love and encouragement into her heart, asking Jesus to begin to heal the inner pain – especially the loss of relatives who had been killed. We asked her to forgive those who had been responsible for the accident. We told the spirits of fear and infirmity, who were confining the body in the same symptoms some thirty years later, to leave.

There was a deep deliverance and a profound healing. Normal movement in the woman's neck was restored and for the first time for as long as she could remember she could breathe deeply once again. She knew that asthma was a thing of the past. God had healed her of the trauma on the inside, leaving her body free to receive the healing that she was longing for.

We have seen hundreds of people healed in this way. When God heals us on the inside, then we are free to receive His healing on the outside.

When Trauma Goes Unresolved

Finally, just a word about those who begin to suffer physically because of unresolved trauma and inner pain. When, for example, a mother receives news of the sudden death of her child in a road accident, the mother has not suffered physically at all. But the inner pain is immense and it is through our body that we actually express the pain – often through seasons of tears and even, in a case as severe as this, wailing. But for some people, such news is so traumatic that they are unable to cope with the shock. The heart is broken, the pain is never expressed, and it all gets locked away on the inside. The inner grief, which is a consequence of the trauma, begins to affect the physical well-being. It is now being said by some medics that they believe unresolved grief can even be a primary cause of cancer.

One lady with a broken heart shared with me how her young daughter had died in a fire. She described the burning house so vividly that I assumed this had only just happened. But when I asked for more information, I discovered her daughter had died fourteen years previously. If God had not come to her on that night and mended her broken heart, she would have lived the rest of her days in a heartbroken, traumatized condition. Who knows what the secondary physical consequences might have been?

Unresolved trauma lies at the root of far more sickness and infirmity than perhaps anyone has previously understood. It is so important that we allow the Lord to heal us on the inside as well as ask Him for healing on the outside!

Chapter Six

Mending Cracks in the Soul

Dale M. Sides

Dale is founder and president of Liberating Ministries for Christ International. With over 30 years of ministry experience, Dale travels and speaks extensively throughout the United States and abroad. He is the author of numerous books including *Mending Cracks in the Soul* and *God Damn Satan!*. Dale also holds several degrees, including a Doctorate of Theology in Religious Education from Andersonville Baptist Seminary. He and his wife, Vicki, live with their four daughters in Bedford, Virginia. To learn more about his ministry or available resources, phone 540-586-5813 or visit www.LMCI.org.

The body lacerates, bruises, or breaks because of the force of an object on it, but the soul cracks due to trauma and emotional overload. A crack in someone's soul is often a much more severe injury than one to the body. If not treated properly, it could result in a warped personality much the same as if a broken bone were not set and grew back crooked.

An emotionally wounded individual is complicated but the problem is compounded by the fact that demons can enter into people at times of trauma. For example, one of the most dysfunctional characters in the whole Bible is the madman of Gadara. It is apparent that he had demons and that the demons had to be cast out, but the conclusion of his deliverance was that he was clothed, seated, and *in his right mind.*

Yes, the demons were a problem, but how they got in was the fundamental problem. He had a crack in his soul that allowed demons to come in and, consequently, this was the last item that needed to be fixed (Mark 5:15). The emphasis of this account is not the demons but the deliverance that came through Jesus to this man. Do not despair, these issues can be fixed *if* we recognize that there is a problem and refer to the Word of God as our textbook for treatment. The bottom line is this: If we do not fix the crack whereby the demons came in, we will have to do the deliverance again.

Therefore, my aim in writing this portion of *Ministering Freedom to the Emotionally Wounded* is to give the remedy for fixing the crack where the demons enter. I also want to cover some biblical text documenting this type of healing. But my main emphasis is to show how the Holy Spirit works with you to repair the crack and, once and for all, close the access portal to demons.

Before beginning, I would like to emphasize that mending this crack is a two-part remedy. This is like epoxy glue. It has two parts: One is a filler and the other is a hardener. One without the other looks like it might work—and even may work for a very short duration—but when both of them are used the crack will be filled in and will be healed to the point of *no scar*. The Holy Spirit provides the initial action of identifying the place of injury and filling in the crack with truth; but the Bible, held and confessed over and over is the hardener that will complete the process.

The Biblical Proof

Luke 4:18 verifiably testifies that the Holy Spirit was upon Jesus to heal the brokenhearted. Moreover, it says that He came to set at liberty those who have been bruised. As we more closely examine the word "bruised," we will see the actual promise in the Word of God to heal those who have been traumatized.

Bruised from Luke 4:18 is the Greek word *thrauo* (Strong's #2352). The definition means to shatter or break in pieces. So, literally this promise says that the Holy Spirit has a ministry to set at liberty those who have been broken or cracked. Furthermore, its root word is akin to the word for "wounds" in Luke 10:34: "And went to him, and bound up his *wounds*, pouring in oil and wine, and set him on his own beast, and brought him to an inn, and took care of him" (KJV, emphasis mine).

The word for wounds here is the Greek word *trauma*— literally trauma. Putting this together, we see the promise of God that the Good Samaritan, Jesus Christ, will heal your trauma through the ministry of the Holy Spirit. In addition, Luke 10:34 says that Jesus will heal the wound (trauma) by pouring in oil and wine. The oil and wine shows the two-part remedy. The oil represents the ministry of the Holy Spirit and wine refers to the Word of God, specifically regarding forgiveness through the blood of Jesus.

I have literally seen thousands of people revived in hope by seeing these verses—because faith comes from hearing the Word of God (Romans 10:17). They realize that this is not just a ploy but a living and vital promise from God Almighty to those who have been struggling under dysfunctions of fear, worry, rejection, abandonment, anger, lust, pride, etc. To paraphrase this truth: God Almighty says, "Jesus came to heal your broken heart of trauma. Through the Holy Spirit and the Word of God, He can put the pieces of your heart together again." Praise God!

From Luke 4:18, we have seen that the Holy Spirit heals the brokenhearted. From doing a simple word search where "heal" and "heart" are used in the same verse, we discover how the Holy Spirit will find and heal this crack. Matthew 13:15, John 12:40, and Acts 28:27 have these words in them and they all refer back to Isaiah 6:10. A single verse quoted three separate times shows a magnificent truth. This truth is *how* a broken heart is healed. "For this people's heart is waxed gross, and their ears are dull of hearing, and their eyes they have closed; lest at any time they should see with their eyes and hear with their ears, and should understand with their heart, and should be converted, and I should heal them" (Matthew 13:15, KJV).

This verse says that if we can see with the true eyes and ears of our heart, or spirit, that we can be converted and healed. "Converted" is the Greek word *epistrepho*, which means to "twist back" or "untwist." This verse tells us that if we can see with the eyes and ears of the spirit that we can untwist our souls and have our broken heart healed. As we follow this backwards in Scripture, we see the first usage of the eyes being opened, or as we shall see, eyes being closed. This search leads us back to Genesis 3, the fall of humanity.

Seeing with the Real Eyes

What causes a trauma is when we view the situation with our physical eyes instead of our spiritual eyes. *The key to having our trauma healed is to view the situation with our spiritual eyes instead of the eyes of the flesh.*

The serpent said to Eve in Genesis 3:5 that if she ate of the tree of knowledge of good and evil that her eyes would be opened. In fact, in Genesis 3:7 it says that their eyes were opened. So, did the devil lie? Yes. But we must understand that the devil's preference in lies is deception and telling part truths. Notice that Genesis 3:7 says that their eyes were opened *and* they knew they were naked. So, in reality, the eyes of their flesh were opened because they lost the true vision of their spiritual eyes.

Viewing traumatic situations with the physical eyes is what causes us to fear because we fear death. We can be overwhelmed with emotional sensations to the end that our souls crack under the strain of emotional pressure. Emotions are wonderful aspects of our soul. They are the spice of life, but too much spice causes "heartburn." Likewise, emotions are good if taken in moderation, but when you accidentally dump the whole salt container on your chicken cordon bleu, you have a mess. You either throw the chicken away or scrape the

> It is quite possible to cast the demons out of the person, but if the memory of the initial event is not healed or the crack repaired, the possibility of the demons returning is very high.

salt off of it. When emotions are heaped upon you due to fear of the physical flesh dying or being punished, your soul can crack under the strain.

When the crack occurs, demons, being either the perpetrators of the event or capitalizing on it, enter the "opened mind." Once they are in the person, when a similar or associated event occurs and the same emotion erupts, the demons take control of that portion of the brain and make the person think the way the demons want them to think. The demons hide in the abnormal emotion.

It is quite possible to cast the demons out of the person, but if the memory of the initial event is not healed or the crack repaired, the possibility of the demons returning is very high. So the issue is not just to cast out the demons, but to heal the crack so that the demons cannot get back in.

How Is the Crack Healed?

The key to mending cracks in the soul is for the Holy Spirit to take you backwards in your memory and show you what was happening in the spirit realm at the time of the trauma. This is called "opening the eyes of your heart or spirit." Look at this account where the spiritual eyes were opened:

"And Elisha prayed, and said, LORD, I pray thee, open his eyes, that he may see. And *the LORD opened the eyes of the young man;* and he saw: and, behold, the mountain was full of horses and chariots of fire round about Elisha" (2 Kings 6:17, KJV, emphasis mine).

The promise is in the New Testament as well:

"That the God of our Lord Jesus Christ, the Father of glory, may give unto you the spirit of wisdom and revelation in the knowledge of him: *The eyes of your understanding [heart] being enlightened...*" (Ephesians 1:17,18a, KJV, emphasis mine).

The Holy Spirit can open the eyes of our spirit and overwrite the fear and trauma we have experienced. We have been missing a tremendous truth about the Holy Spirit being able to show us things from the past. We often only think about the possibilities of the Holy Spirit showing us things in the future (John 16:13), but He can also show us things in the past. For example, He took Moses backwards and showed him the revelation of things that happened before him as is recorded in the book of Genesis. Likewise, the Holy Spirit took Luke backwards and showed him the details of the book of Acts.

This is the key to having trauma healed: the Holy Spirit takes you back into the trauma and shows you what was happening in the spirit realm at the time of the incident. *He overwrites trauma with truth.* You realize the truth when you see with your real eyes (eyes of the spirit).

For example, a lady came to me for ministry. She was having panic attacks while in heavy traffic. She would become so afraid that she would have to pull off the road until the traffic subsided. When I ministered to her, I simply asked the Holy Spirit to take her back in her memory to the incident where she was traumatized and the door was opened for this spirit of fear to come in. Almost immediately, she said, "I am five years old and in the car with my mother." She continued, "Another car pulls out in front of us and we hit it. My mother is flying through the windshield. Oh God," she said, "We are going to die."

At that point, I asked the Holy Spirit to open the eyes of her spirit and show her what was happening during the event. It was just like the prayer that Elisha prayed for his servant to see the spirit realm—except the Spirit took her backward. The lady gasped and said, "Who is that very large man sitting in the seat next to me, with his arm around me?" I said, "That is the angel of the Lord's presence protecting you!" She said, "Has he always been there?" "Yes," I said. "He was there that day and that is why you did not fly through the windshield too."

Once the fear was dispelled and the hiding place of the demon was discovered, I simply said to the demon, "Spirit of fear, go in Jesus' name! You have no place to hide." The lady let out a moan and breathed the spirit out of her body." She has never been plagued with panic attacks since.

The root or anchor point of the emotion of fear was re-moved when she saw the angel. Now when she is in traffic, or in any other place that is conducive to fear, the emotion of fear has no place to default to so she does not register the initial trauma or the effect of it. Since the demon is gone, she is in control of her own mind and will.

I gave her verses of Scripture to "harden" the filler of the Holy Spirit. 2 Timothy 1:7 and Hebrews 13:5b have become memory strongholds for her. Anytime she feels fear coming upon her she *verbalizes* these verses. I have seen individuals healed of fear, anger, lust, rejection, sexual maladies, eating disorders, shame, etc., and I am continually amazed at the de-liverance people have.

Quote the Word

Demons cannot read your mind, so when they return, they will speak to you and try to get you to verbalize an opening. Instead of saying what they want you to say, do what Jesus did. He quoted the Word of God—verbatim, word for word with the volume and accompanying faith that sent chills up the devil's spine.

There is kinetic power in the Bible. It is released into the senses realm as active energy when it comes out of the mouth of a saint of God. Actually, according to Psalm 103:20, angels hearken to the commandment of God when they hear the voice of the Lord. Since the Holy Spirit is working in you, when you speak the Bible, angels obey your word just as they obeyed Jesus' word when He was physically on this planet.

Holy Scripture has energy that is released when it comes out of your mouth. Quote the Word of God and add hardener to the patch that the Holy Spirit has fixed in your soul.

Conclusion

The promises of God are always true. He sent the Holy Spirit to help you cure the dysfunctions of your past by removing the lie of emotional imbalance. The lie is removed when the Holy Spirit shows you what happened in the spirit realm when the trauma took place. He overwrites trauma with truth. Once the truth has been sown in your mind, as you quote Bible verses related to the remedy, the patch thoroughly "cures."

God does not want you to live dysfunctionally because of old, ugly memories. Truth overwrites trauma when the Holy Spirit causes you to realize the truth through the "real eyes" of the spirit. Once you have seen the truth, build your mental and emotional strength by quoting the written Scriptures.

Truth overwrites trauma, heals broken hearts, balances emotions, and cures dysfunction. The truth comes from the Spirit of Truth and the Word of Truth. It is a two-part remedy.

Jesus, the Good Samaritan, pours in the oil of the Holy Spirit and the wine of the Word of God. Jesus came to heal the brokenhearted and to set at liberty those who have been traumatized.

Subject Index

Look for other books in this series!

The Proven Foundations for Deliverance series continues with five more watershed books. Doris M. Wagner assembles top ministry practitioners to address specific topics of deliverance. Other books include:

Book One: Ministering Freedom from Demonic Oppression

Issues addressed include:
- The biblical basis for deliverance
- Can a Christian have a demon?
- Satan's plan to divert us from the path of God
- The believer's authority over demonic spirits
- How to minister spiritual housecleaning
- Deliverance in the local church
- How deliverance sustains revival

Book Three: Ministering Freedom to the Sexually Broken (Coming in Summer, 2003)

Issues addressed include:
- Ministering to the sexually abused and traumatized
- Promiscuity: fornication, adultery, and prostitution
- Aftermath of abortion
- Homosexuality
- Childhood Sexual Trauma
- Pornography and sexual addictions
- Teens Dealing with Lust

Book Four: Ministering Freedom to Family Issues (Coming in Late Fall, 2003)

Issues addressed include:

- Ministering to childhood issues including adopted, unwanted, and wrong-sex children
- Abuses and addictions within the home
- Fatherlessness
- Divorce
- How to minister deliverance to a child
- Praying for teens
- Autism Spectrum Disorder and ADHD

Book Five: Ministering Freedom from the Occult (Coming in Spring, 2004)

Issues addressed include:

- The occult and youth
- Witchcraft
- Curses and blessings
- Freemasonry, Voodoo, Santaria
- Ritualistic abuse in multiple personality disorder
- Common occult practices including New Age, hypnosis, certain martial arts, etc.

Book Six: Practical Keys for Conducting a Deliverance Session (Coming in Fall, 2004)

In this book, several seasoned deliverance practitioners will share effective methods and models for conducting a deliverance session.

(Please note: Titles, issues addressed, and release dates are subject to change.)